FINANCIAL RESCUE: THE TOTAL MONEY MAKEOVER

CREATE WEALTH, REDUCE DEBT & GAIN FREEDOM

CASSANDRA GAISFORD

BLUE GIRAFFE PUBLISHING

PRAISE FOR FINANCIAL RESCUE: THE TOTAL MONEY MAKEOVER

"Financial Rescue: The Total Money Makeover is a perfect financial pocket rocket.

This book allowed me to explore and review my financial position without fear, anxiety or self-ickyness. The wonderful thing about reading this book is that it has given me the tools and knowledge to gain a clear picture of where I stand financially, and I now have greater confidence to approach my bank for a financial maintenance meeting.

I have a list of topics I wish to discuss with my bank and language appropriate. The author's fun and intelligent book is for each and every one of us seeking knowledge on developing our clarity on our financial position, or looking for the confidence to explore other options with our bank or for those who want the language of the everyday financial world. "

~ Catherine Sloan, counselor

"Financial help for creatives! I enjoyed this book very much. Filled with practical information and ideas that will put more money in your pockets, *Financial Rescue* is a guide for finding financial freedom."

~ **Courtney Kenney, author of** *Creating Space to Thrive: Get Unstuck, Reboot Your Creativity and Change Your Life.*

INTRODUCTION

You may not have the cash at the moment, and the economy may not be ideal, but that doesn't mean your mind can't be working on your ideas and creating the way to a better future. Look for opportunities in every climate. That's leverage.
~ Cassandra Gaisford

As I update this book the world is in the midst of the COVID-19 crisis. Millions of lives and careers have been disrupted and incomes severed—some disappearing permanently.

Now, more than ever, we all have to reinvent our lives and many of us many feel we have no money to give us the kick-start we need. My hope is that in the pages that follow you'll discover a few strategies to help you find spare cash,, overcome obstacles, stress less and whip your finances into shape.

Many people dream of changing careers, or writing a book or making a living from their passion. But too often an economic crisis and lack of spare cash is holding them back.

Perhaps you can identify with what one of my clients in

her fifties said to me recently, "I'd love to change careers if my mortgage would let me."

She, and others like her, who feel trapped by debt and financial constraints, prevent themselves from choosing what they want to do because they fear there won't be the necessary money or support to allow it.

But money worries don"t have to be an obstacle to seeking more fulfilling work. Financing a career change, despite all the obstacles in your way, involves a conscious commitment to move forward, and a willingness to think laterally and pragmatically about a range of financial options.

There are many different ways to finance a career change including: consolidating debt, future-gazing and demand creation, career combo-ing, seeking investors, using equity, reducing outgoings, generating extra cash flow, and applying for funding.

The discipline needed to reprioritise your finances will be easier, and the sacrifices more bearable, if you allow your desire to drive you.

Let's take a closer look at some of the possible financing options.

DEDICATION

*I dedicate this book to those of you
who are ready to live a beautiful life,
to stress less and do what others may say cannot be done.*

*This book is also for Lorenzo, my Knight Templar,
who encourages and supports me
to make my dreams possible...*

*And for all my clients
who've shared their dreams with me,
and allowed me to help them achieve amazing feats.*

Thank you for inspiring me.

AUTHOR'S NOTE

The Art of Business

I first made a significant income starting my life and career coaching consultancy, Worklife Solutions. Prior to this I was a single mom struggling to make ends meet and trapped in a soul-sucking day job that gave me shingles and eroded by confidence and self-esteem.

I share my experience of finding my mojo and making an awesome living in my *Mid-Life Career Rescue* series.

It's my successful experience as a businesswoman and creative entrepreneur that I bring to my writing, and which I want to share with you. I've learned that it is vitally important to treat writing, or any other creative skill from which you wish to make a living, as a business.

As Sir Richard Branson, English business magnate and founder of Virgin Records, notes, "Building a business is not rocket science, it's about having a great idea and seeing it through with integrity."

My *one thing* is to live and create with passion and purpose. And to help others achieve the same. With this guiding light, I have created multiple streams of income—many of them from my writing. Others from my art.

I've also developed other income streams from my work as a holistic therapist, life and career coach, mentor to creatives. And from certifying people to become location-independent Worklife Solutions life, career, and courage coaches.

People write to me and tell me that they are awed by my prosperous productivity and success. But I feel it's so important to let you know that I wasn't always the confident, prosperous author and business woman I am today.

For many years I struggled to pay my bills. I wrestled unsuccessfully with debt, anxiety and fear and other blocks to living a prosperous life.

Because of my own limiting beliefs about my ability to be independently wealthy, it took me until my forties to realise many of my dreams.

Even then I struggled. I hadn't gone to university and received an English degree. I didn't train as a journalist. Everything I learned was self-taught in the University of Life. It took me many years to value this.

Happily, I'm a compulsive note-taker and researcher—my partner once said that I'm an obsessive collector of positivity. My goal has always been to overcome obstacles and live my best life—and to help people like you achieve the same.

Your Virtual Mentor

Whenever I'm in a slump or needing an inspirational boost, I turn to people who are smarter or more skilled than me for good advice. Very often, I write a book—like this one, to self-help my way to greater prosperity.

If you've been feeling fearful, anxious, despondent or

depressed—or just getting in your own way, you're in good company. I've been there, too—as have many successful people. Getting in your own way is normal!

I promise there are solutions to the financial challenges you're currently facing—and you'll find them in the pages that follow.

Much of the wisdom contained in this book, and in *Developing a Millionaire Mindset*, the first in The Prosperous Author series, are the success strategies I've distilled and applied in the last few years.

What changed?

My mindset, and my systemic effectiveness and purposeful productivity amongst other things.

What You'll Discover

In *Financial Rescue: The Total Money Makeover*, I'll share with you the things I've learned figuring out how to make a living from my passions.

You'll benefit from dozens of insights based on survey research and my professional achievements as a holistic psychologist, bestselling author, and creativity expert.

You'll gain insight into the success secrets of extraordinary authors and creative entrepreneurs from a variety of fiction and non-fiction genres. Tim Ferriss, James Patterson, Paulo Coelho, Nora Roberts, Arianna Huffington, Oprah, and Isabel Allende are just a few of the many creative mentors you'll learn from.

As you'll discover, being prosperous is not just about money; it's also about health, happiness, close relationships, living a meaningful life, and enjoying life's journey.

As one advance reader wrote to me: "I'm emailing you to let you know the impact your book has had on me. I cold-turkey stopped imbibing alcohol and coke and I've gained twenty years in energy. We all know we don't drink a lot but what an insidious thing nightly alcohol is...Thank you for your book - it's become a bit of a bible, or should I say they've become bits of bibles."

I'm so pleased to know this! It's amazing how much more easily it is to reduce debt and boost your income is gained by making changes to your health habits.

With *Financial Rescue: The Total Money Makeover: Create Wealth, Reduce Debt & Gain Freedom,* you'll be able to:

- Stress less and whip your finances into shape
- Find a way to finance a career change and create a living from your passions
- Design a sure-fire plan for paying off all debt
- Overcome mindset issues, including self-doubt, fear of failure, anxiety, or despair
- Boost confidence or self-esteem
- Employ creative strategies and scientifically engineered hacks proven to increase prosperity
- Do less and earn more
- Apply no-hype, practical tips and easily implementable strategies
- Create a big, fat nest egg for emergencies and retirement!

. . . then *Financial Rescue: The Total Money Makeover* is exactly the right book for you. It will show you that these challenges, obstacles, and desires are a critical part of your success.

The ideas described in this book apply to anyone who's trying to inject some purposeful prosperity into their life and work.

In short, this book is for you—whoever you are, whatever your financial situation, and however you define prosperity.

Your Living Guide to Success

Like all good things, this book is organic. If you feel something is missing, or you want to share your success strategy, please write to me. I'll be updating the content regularly and sharing additional tips on my blog.

1
CULTIVATE HOPE

One's thoughts turn towards hope.

~ Leonardo da Vinci

No matter what your situation, how dire your debt, how impossible finding a solution seems, always, always retain hope.

Take comfort from other "failures"—love them, or not, some of the wealthiest people today have found their way back from homelessness, bankruptcy and despair. Donald Trump, J.K. Rowling and Chris Gardner (think, Will Smith in *The Pursuit of Happyness*) are just some of many, many successful stories of transformational change.

Common obstacles to achieving the same success in your own situation include victim-thinking, fear, self-doubt, and other crippling thoughts. But what if all you had to do to tame these "uglies" was to cultivate hope?

The power of hope is grounded firmly in spiritual and

religious practices but also in science. Like the ancient Greeks and Romans, Leonardo da Vinci, and even 18th-century physicians, recognised the physiological effects of mind-power and hope on the body.

Successful medical outcomes, even when the intervention is a placebo, further evidence the impact of maintaining a positive expectation.

Dr. Joe Dispenza powerfully illustrates this fact in his fabulous book *You Are the Placebo: Making Your Mind Matter*.

If like me, and Joe Dispenza, you've manifested miracles in your own life by maintaining a positive expectation, you'll know the power of hope.

Thoughts *do* become things. Scientists Gregg Braden and Bruce Lipton, author of *The Biology of Belief*, have evidenced this.

But hope can only flourish when you believe that what you do can make a difference, that you recognise that you have choices and that your actions can create a future which differs from your present situation.

When you empower your belief in your ability to gain some control over your circumstances, you are no longer entirely at the mercy of forces outside yourself. You are back in the driving seat.

"Fearlessness is like a muscle. I know from my own life that the more I exercise it the more natural it becomes to not let my fears run me," says businesswoman, author, and founder of *The Huffington Post*, Arianna Huffington.

Would you rather be a failure at something you love than a failure at something you hate? It's a question worth considering.

What you believe has a tremendous influence on the likelihood of success. Reframe your fears and buoy your dreams with hope. Not "I'm afraid of failing," but "I hope to succeed," or something similar. And set your eyes firmly on a target you want to achieve. We'll dive deeper into these success strategies, including the power of audacious obsession in this book.

Hope is the foundation from which all else follows—nurture a sense of positive expectancy. Fake it until you make it. More on this later....

How could you cultivate more hope? If you felt the fear and did it anyway, what's the best that could happen?

Check out my blog for 21 ways to turn your thoughts to hope—http://bit.ly/29NiQU5hope.

2

PLAN FOR SUCCESS—SET AND ACHIEVE GOALS

Remember, dreams without goals are just dreams and they ultimately fuel disappointment. Have dreams, but have goals, life goals, yearly goals, monthly goals, daily goals.

~ Denzel Washington, actor

"Luck is preparation meeting opportunity," Oprah once said.

Planning and effort prevents poor performance—this is such a powerful message when it comes to your financial goals, especially if you're someone who equates planning with feeling controlled.

You may be like many people who look to the future thinking, "Someday! Someday I will achieve that."

How can you be assured that things will happen if you don't plan your action steps effectively, efficiently, and productively?

So many people end their lives disappointed that things didn't come to fruition. "Why didn't it happen for me?" they say. "My life is a life of regret."

Successful people don't sit at home waiting for things to happen. They go out and conquer things.

If you're sitting back waiting for "someday" you have a problem—you think you have time!

What is your current planning mindset? Do you plan your life by:

- Beginning with the end in mind—planning at least five to ten years ahead, and working back to ensure that everything you do now moves you ahead?
- Creating outcome-focused goals?
- Or, just going with the flow and trusting the Universe or Providence to deliver?

There's a time for planning and a time to create, seize, and act upon opportunities. It's a balancing act. Whatever your approach, plan to make your success a reality. Your efforts will be repaid in exchange for your labor and your commitment to plan and persevere.

"I try to give myself a goal every day," says Denzel Washington. "Sometimes, it's just to not curse somebody out. Simple goals. But have goals and understand to achieve these goals you must apply discipline and consistency. In order to achieve your goals, you must apply discipline and consistency every day—not just on Tuesday and then miss a few days. You have to work at it every day.

"You have to plan every day. You've heard the saying 'We don't plan to fail, we fail to plan.' Hard work works. Working really hard is what successful people do. In this text, tweet, twerk world that you've grown up in, remember just because you're doing a lot more doesn't mean you're getting a lot more done."

Jeff Goins, author of *Real Artist's Don't Starve*, said he sets himself the smallest achievable goal possible. Committing to writing 500 new words every day, he says, boosts confidence as he knows it's achievable.

"Resistance is trying to keep you from being your best self. So I get up and work out, then I come home, make my kids breakfast, then I take my son to school," said Goins in an interview with Joanna Penn.

Listen to his interview on Joanna Penn's Podcast: https://www.thecreativepenn.com/2017/07/17/real-artists-dont-starve-jeff-goins/

Rewrite your goals

List all the benefits making a change will bring. These may include better health, more money in the longer term or improved relationships with loved ones.

3
WHAT DO YOU BELIEVE?

A large income is the best recipe for happiness I have heard of.

~ Jane Austen

"Research shows that 80 percent of individuals will never be financially free in the way they'd like to be, and 80 percent will never claim to be truly happy," writes T. Harv Eker in his book *Secrets of the Millionaire Mind: Mastering the Inner Game of Wealth*.

"The reason is simple," Eker writes, "Most people are unconscious. They are a little asleep at the wheel. They work and think on a superficial level of life—based only on what they can see. They live strictly in the visible world."

Yet, many of the things that influence your thoughts, feelings, and behaviours are invisible; a great many lurk in the realm of the subconscious mind.

The function of your subconscious mind is to store and retrieve data. Its job is to ensure that you respond exactly the way you are programmed.

"By the time you reach the age of 21, you've already permanently stored more than one hundred times the contents of the entire Encyclopaedia Britannica," says motivational writer Brian Tracy.

And much of this information is rubbish, false, incomplete, or obsolete.

REPROGRAMMING Your Subconscious Beliefs

Your subconscious mind is like a huge memory bank. Its capacity is virtually unlimited. It permanently stores everything that ever happens to you. What is limited is your ability to consciously recall many of the scripts programmed into your mind.

You may not even be aware of limiting beliefs that are holding you back or placing a cap on your ability to earn a living from your writing.

One of the most important things you can commit to realising is that you exist in more than the physical world. The mental world, the emotional world, and the spiritual world all exert a powerful influence over you—whether you are consciously tapping into them or not.

"What most people never realise is that the physical realm is merely a 'printout' of the other three," writes T. Harv Eker.

Any limiting and unhelpful beliefs or repressed experiences preventing you from becoming a prosperous author cannot be changed in the physical world. They can only be changed in the "program"—the mental, emotional, and spiritual worlds.

Which is why *Financial Rescue: The Total Money Makeover* takes a holistic approach to success. Passion, joy, faith, prayer, dreams, purpose, and mindfulness practices are some of the strategies we'll discuss in this book.

You'll also learn how to develop a rock-solid belief in your ability to succeed. Building firm self-confidence will help you beat the nay-sayers and weather the inevitable setbacks with ease.

4

YOUR MONEY BLUEPRINT

It's not enough to be in the right place at the right time. You have to be the right person in the right place at the right time.

~ T. Harv Eker, author

Your financial blueprint consists of a combination of your thoughts, feelings, and actions related to money.

It's formed primarily during childhood and the information or "programming" you received in the past. Imprinted upon you by parents, siblings, friends, authority figures, teachers, religious leaders, media, your culture, and other influential sources later in life, your beliefs, you sometimes find, are mistaken.

You may have heard, as I did growing up, that you'll never make a living from art. Or that art doesn't contribute anything of value to society.

The chances are high that you were actively discouraged and channeled into supposedly more "prosperous" or socially sanctioned pursuits, like being a lawyer or a doctor —or a good wife!

As Jeff Goins notes, for years, the fallacy of the starving artist has pervaded our culture, leaching into the minds of creative people and stifling their dreams.

But the evidence-based truth is that the world's most successful authors and artists do not starve. They thrive by leveraging off the power of their millionaire mindset and by capitalising on their creative strengths.

Your thoughts and what you believe to be true for you influences your feelings, your energy, and ultimately your behaviour.

What you believe, consciously or unconsciously, sets your income threshold.

Prosperous people are never content with just scraping by. They believe they have the potential to create unlimited wealth—and they set out to achieve it.

So who are you? How do you think? What are your beliefs? What are your habits and traits? How do you really feel about money and your earning potential?

Answering these initial questions, and those below, will help your journey toward prosperity. You'll learn more strategies to help boost your self-awareness and co-create new liberating beliefs throughout this book.

5

WHAT'S BLOCKING YOUR PROSPERITY?

Your lifestyle does affect your work and as long as you have the wrong life schedule your productivity will not achieve its maximum potential.

~ *Jessica Mills, blog editor*

How productive are you? Do you know who or what gets in the way of your prosperous productivity?

Many people unfairly blame writer's block when they fail to write consistently or churn out their books in awe-inspiring time.

But very often an underlying, unresolved or unacknowledged fear is to blame for a lack of prosperous productivity. Fear of success, fear of failure, fear of attracting attention, fear of criticism and other worries can put a real damper on prosperous productivity.

Or perhaps it is the fear of disappointing family members and loved ones who are happy for you to pursue a writing career as long as their life doesn't change in the interim.

"Do the thing you fear and the death of fear is certain," author Susan Jeffers once wrote. This may require saying "No" to others' insistent demands on your time.

Or, "No" to your own self-sabotaging behaviours—something we'll dive deeper into further in this book.

Just how to summon the courage or conviction to do this can be challenging. If your mindset needs a fine-tune I encourage you to revisit book one of The Prosperity for Authors series, *Developing a Millionaire Mindset*.

However, what if you don't know what or who is to blame for your poor productivity?

Naming and, if appropriate, shaming your productivity blocks will help you develop a winning strategy.

How many of the following common barriers to productivity apply to you:

- Distraction
- Lack of focus
- Unclear priorities
- Self-limiting beliefs
- Negative self-talk
- Drama/toxic relationships
- "Shiny object" syndrome
- Perfectionism
- Disorganisation/clutter
- Juggling responsibilities
- Stress
- Lack of sleep
- Television/gaming/social media
- Your lifestyle/life schedule
- Something or someone else…

A GREAT WAY TO redress any imbalance is to ask yourself the following questions:

"How does (perfectionism, for example) help or hinder my prosperous productivity?"

"What's the one thing I can do such that by doing it everything else will be easier or unnecessary?"

6

MONITOR YOUR PROSPEROUS PRODUCTIVITY

What gets measured gets done—or does it?

~ Forbes Magazine

You can't improve your productivity effectively if you don't have information you can use to make decisions to improve your results. The question is—are you measuring what really matters?

If you're serious about clearing debt, or making a living from your passion, treat it like a business. Manage for success by identifying and listing your Key Performance Indicators (KPI's).

These may include the debt you want to reduce, income you want to generate and the tasks needed to complete them. You may also find value in monitoring activities that sustain prosperous productivity, including down-time and well-being related activities.

Keep a watchful and protective eye on your prosperous productivity. You may find, as I once did, creating an excel sheet and both blocking time and recording how you spent it during the week helps clarify where the productivity leaks are occurring. Once you know this you can begin to develop a winning strategy.

Increased accountability and a competitive drive to succeed are added benefits of including stretch goals and monitoring your results.

The term "eustress" refers to "good stress," or the opposite of distress, and captures that healthy response to stress we have when something is attainable, but almost too far out of research.

A *Forbes Magazine* article highlights research showing that the desire to win is heightened when rivalry and time pressure coincide, "and the simple act of measuring something sparks that sense of rivalry in many people."

That rivalry doesn't need to be with others, it can be with your own self as you compete to see whether you can achieve and beat a goal that may have seemed unobtainable.

"Without a measure, there is no way to determine whether you have won, and therefore, less motivation to get something done."

Then there's that small matter of accountability. When you set goals and measure performance against that goal, you increase the ability to hold yourself (and others) accountable for the resulting success or failure.

This concrete data spotlights what you did or didn't do, what the impact was, and provides clues to what you need to do differently.

Design **Your Data to Tell a Story**

Once the right data is measured and collected, make information eye-catching, visual and interesting to highlight the most important points and make it easier to see what's going on.

To make monitoring and managing my debt reduction and prosperous productivity fun and creative and efficient, I developed a colour-coded weekly spreadsheet for my most important projects, stretch goals and common responsibilities.

On this sheet I record books in progress, relationship priorities, health and well-being goals and more mundane tasks that require my time.

In this way, I both record and block out my time efficiently and effectively. It's easy to see how well I've done and where I need to improve when I do my end of week, end of month, end of quarter etc reviews.

What are your most critical measurements of success or Key Performance Indicators?

How can you measure and monitor your progress and hold yourself accountable?

7

THE POWER OF PASSION

Of all strata of the pyramid, passion is the most important for your soul and, almost always, your ultimate success.

~ James Scott Bell, author

"Nothing great in the world has been accomplished without passion," the philosopher G.W.F. Hegel once said. Denzel Washington and many other successful creative people agree. "You only live once, so do what you feel passionate about, take chances professionally, don't be afraid to fail," Washington says.

- Passion is energy. Without energy, you have nothing.
- To be passionate is to be fully alive.
- Passion is about emotion, feeling, zest, and enthusiasm.

- Passion is about intensity, fervour, ardor, and zeal.
- Passion is about fire.
- Passion is about eagerness and preoccupation.
- Passion is about excitement and animation.
- Passion is about determination and self-belief.
- Passion, like love and joy, is contagious.
- Passion can't be faked. It's the mark of authenticity.

Passion fuels inner purpose and fires the flames of your imagination. It gives you a reason for living and the confidence and drive to pursue your dreams. Passion enables you to unleash latent forces and God-given talents.

"We each have passions and skills, but you'll see extraordinarily successful people with one intense emotion or one learned ability that shines through, defining them or driving them more than anything else," writes Gary Keller in *The One Thing: The Surprisingly Simple Truth Behind Extraordinary Results*.

"Often, the line between passion and skills can be blurry. That's because they're almost always connected," Keller says.

When you follow your passion, you'll find your sweet spot. You'll be emboldened by love— thus powering your creativity, courage, resolve, and tenacity. You'll also bounce back from setbacks, and refuse to allow failure to stop you— increasing your likelihood of achieving extraordinary success.

Focus on what excites you. "I find things I like and I do them," says James Patterson, arguably one of the most financially successful authors today.

J.K. Rowling, and other debt-strapped creatives have successfully turned their passion into financial alchemy.

Feel the power that comes from focusing on what excites you, and identify ways following your enthusiasms could make you debt-free.

8

BECOME AUDACIOUSLY OBSESSED

When you are inspired by some great purpose, some extraordinary project, all your thoughts break their bonds. Your mind transcends limitations, your consciousness expands in every direction, and you find yourself in a new, great and wonderful world. Dormant forces, faculties, and talents become alive, and you discover yourself to be a greater person by far than you ever dreamed yourself to be.

~ Patanjali, yogi and mystic

Passionate Obsessions Empower Your Productivity and Prosperity

A healthy obsession can lead you to many things, including:

- A state of divine flow—enabling you to write with mind-blowing productivity

- Your point of excellence—unleashing dormant talents and natural gifts
- Rocket-fuel tenacity to persevere and succeed
- Mentors, helpful allies and similarly obsessed people who will cheerlead and elevate your success
- A legion of devoted fans who are drawn to your impassioned writing
- Your passion and life purpose—spreading seeds of joy and inspiration and benefiting others
- Your life niche—creating a breath of fresh air and giving you a competitive edge
- True bliss—leading you to your vocation where being paid is the icing on the cake

NEW ZEALAND MOTORCYCLING legend Burt Munro proved that passionate obsession is the key to success. "All my life I've wanted to do something big," he said. In 1967 Burt achieved something huge.

At the age of 68, against all the odds, he set a world record of 183.586 mph with his highly modified Indian Scout motorcycle. To qualify he made a one-way run of 190.07 mph, the fastest ever officially recorded speed on an Indian.

Like for so many inspiring people, the road to success was not an easy one—it involved much personal hardship and numerous setbacks, but armed with his passion and a compelling desire to "go out with a bang," Burt Munro mortgaged his house and set out on the greatest adventure of his life.

His truly awesome achievements were brought to life in an inspiring and uplifting film, *The World's Fastest Indian*.

The World's Fastest Indian not only gives movie-goers an inside look at Munro's passion, but it also gives them an idea of New Zealand filmmaker Roger Donaldson's overwhelming desire to tell the story.

"This project has been a passion of mine since I completed a documentary about Burt Munro back in 1972," Donaldson said. "I have been intrigued by Burt's story for many, many years; some would say my obsession with this film matches Burt's obsession with his bike."

Donaldson's passion for his subject has won him international acclaim from Academy Award-winning actor Anthony Hopkins.

"I thought it was a terrific movie. It is a unique script...it is just so well written, very well written, beautifully written, and so refreshing. I've worked with a lot of great directors, Steven Spielberg and Oliver Stone, and Roger Donaldson is there with that lot, you know. He really is," Hopkins said.

BECOME AUDACIOUSLY OBSESSED in your quest to reduce debt and to create wealth.

"The ambitious are criticised by those that have given up," says multi-millionaire property investor and author Grant Cardone. In this book, "*Be Obsessed or Be Average*," Cardone shares how he channelled negative behaviours and habits into a positive addictive energy to be extraordinarily rich.

"Comfort is a disease. And it's what the media wants you to do. It's definitely what the big pharmaceutical companies want you to do. They want you to get comfortable. All the big money on this planet actually wants you to get comfortable so you just sit back and become a passive spectator in the game of life," Cardone says.

"The single biggest financial mistake I've made was not thinking big enough. I encourage you to go for more than a million. There is no shortage of money on this planet, only a shortage of people thinking big enough."

D️ive D️eeper…

If you're struggling to identify your obsessions, you'll find some handy prompts and true stories in Find Your Passion and Purpose. You'll also find inspiration, including true transformational change stories by people like you in my Mid-Life Career Rescue series.

9

DREAM BIG

Don't set out to write a good thriller. Set out to write a #1 thriller.

~James Patterson, author

It's a funny thing, given that science has barely even begun to explore the real potential of the human mind and how easily we persuade ourselves of its limitations and settle for less...

But as Brian Tracy writes in *Eat That Frog! Get More of the Important Things Done—Today*, "You actually feel happier and more powerful when you start and complete a task... and the bigger the task you start and complete, the better and more elated you feel."

Sadly, too often people buy into the mistaken belief that it's easier and more satisfying to chip away at low-value items. I know—I've done this myself. Big mistake!

You've probably caught yourself thinking about a big

dream, some inspired course of action, and at some point talked yourself down by saying, "I could never do that!"

Or perhaps you've come up with a bright idea about something and then shelved it because somebody said dismissively, "You can't do that!" or "That's crap."

Or perhaps, as I have so often said to myself before applying the principals I shared in Developing a Millionaire Mindset, "I can't do this. I can't write this book. It's too big. Who do I think I am trying to write such a complex book?"

But how do you really know what you are capable of unless you try?

Paulo Coehlo, author of *The Alchemist*, once said: "Know what you want and try to go beyond your own expectations. Improve your dancing, practice a lot, and set a very high goal, one that will be difficult to achieve. Because that is an artist's million: to go beyond one's limits. An artist who desires very little and achieves it has failed in life."

Thinking big demands a long step outside the comfort zone of what you know.

It can feel scary to contemplate stepping out of the space where you feel you know what you're doing and you feel fully in control.

It can feel frightening to explore what it would be like if you were to leave the comfort rut and attempt to climb toward a new summit. You don't know for sure where it will lead. But everyone who's ever made a success of anything started with a big dream.

And you can, too.

Tim Ferriss dreams big by adopting and cherishing his beginner's mind. Rather than succumb to the fear of failure, he changes his mindset and affirms his love of variety and challenge and being a perpetual debutante.

"Think small," encourages Gary Keller in his book *The*

One Thing. "Going small" is ignoring all the things you could do and doing what you should do.

"It's recognising that not all things matter equally and finding the things that matter most. It's a tighter way to connect what you do with what you want. It's realising that extraordinary results are directly determined by how narrow you can make a focus."

When you think too big, achieving success can feel overwhelming, time-consuming, and complicated. Calendars can become overloaded and success starts to feel out of reach. So, people opt out and either quit or settle for less.

"Unaware that big success comes when we do a few things well, they get lost trying to do too much, and in the end accomplish too little," says Keller.

"Over time they lower their expectations, abandon their dreams, and allow their life to get small. This is the wrong thing to make small."

Brian Tracy agrees and reminds us in *Eat That Frog! Get More of the Important Things Done—Today,* "The fact is that the amount of time required to complete an important job is often the same as the time required to do an unimportant job. The difference is that you get a tremendous feeling of pride and satisfaction from the completion of something valuable and significant."

Every extraordinary achievement starts as someone's daydream. Dream big. Fuel your verve—pursue the vision that sparkles. Dream huge but plan small. Baby steps will lead to bigger success.

Become audaciously obsessed. Dedicate your time to important tasks which, when completed, will fill you with pride. Resolve today that you are going to spend increasing amounts of time working in those few areas that can make a real difference in our life and career and less time on lower value activities

Anchor your dreams within your heart and feel as though they are already achieved.

10

SEE THE TRUE VALUE

No, I see myself only playing stringed instruments; I have no use for the clarinet.

~ Jessa Crispin, author

"If what we get doesn't fall in line with what we expect, or if what we get is too disruptive, we can fail to see its value. And so we reject it or send it away," Jessa Crispin writes in her book, *The Creative Tarot: A Modern Guide to an Inspired Life*.

"Like, 'No, I see myself only playing stringed instruments; I have no use for the clarinet.' But maybe the clarinet will open up whole new worlds for you if you are willing to give it a try."

Her words are a powerful reinforcement of the previous chapter and the importance of remaining open to listening to the call of your muse and following your deepest enthusiasms.

Looking back, with the benefit of hindsight, I realise I traded down my dream of writing an art-related historical novel because I convinced myself writing it would be financially too disruptive. Instead, I focused my productivity on writing in a genre which I thought would be easier to write, faster to produce, and which would make me more money.

Big mistake. As I shared in the previous chapter, "Dream Big," working outside my true enthusiasms has taken as much time as that which I could have spent writing in the passion-zone—and while yielding steady-sales, they are nowhere near as mind-blowing as my story with heart has the potential to be.

"No, I see myself only writing romance; I have no use for art-related historical fiction," I told myself, if not consciously, then certainly subconsciously.

As you read these words, you may be pleased to know I'm back on track. I'm going to give my story a chance and apply the principals I've learned in books one and two of my Prosperous Author series to finish it.

And you can, too. Finish your book or dream project with heart. See the true value of that which you cherish most.

As Crispin encourages, "An idea or a new inspiration is trying to make itself known to you, but you are desperately trying not to notice—are you willing to give it a try?"

Begin it, begin it now. Once you actually begin working on a valuable task, inspiration will kick in, the energy of the book will take over, and you will be naturally motivated to continue.

Remind yourself of the true value of your most important projects. It maybe the potential for a massive advance on future book sales, a movie deal, or just the pride and satisfaction of finishing the book you never thought you could write.

Resist the temptation to clear up small things first. Begin your high value projects first and go for gold.

11

HYPNOTIZE YOUR MILLIONAIRE MIND

Hypnosis is the epitome of mind-body medicine. It can enable the mind to tell the body how to react and modify the messages that the body sends to the mind.

~ *New York Times*

To get the tremendous power of your unconscious mind behind your goals you will need to program it for success. A simple and exceedingly effective way to do this is through hypnosis.

"Emotional problems work much more on the 'feeling level' than the 'thinking level' which is why just trying to think differently is so hard," say the UK-based hypnotherapists at Uncommon Knowledge.

"We use hypnosis to help you feel different quickly which then makes you think differently about a situation."

You'll recall in the chapter "What Do You Believe?" that

we discussed how important reprogramming both your thinking and your feeling world is to your success.

You can access hypnosis sessions from the comfort of your home via instant download. But a word of caution first—the Internet is awash with websites which offer hypnosis products and services that have not been created by experienced and qualified professionals. Some of these programs are of limited or no use, while others may do more harm than good.

One of my favourite hypnosis sites is run by the UK-based company Uncommon Knowledge. On their website, www.hypnosisdownloads.com, you'll find a range of self-hypnosis mp3 audios, including *The Millionaire Mindset* program. In their own words, they confirm that the program contains the following six success-shaping sessions:

1) Create Winning Business Ideas—enter a creative space within your mind where the money-making ideas will flow like molten gold.

2) Create Real Business Passion—generate a powerful deep unconscious drive for your business idea that will propel you forward.

3) Build Unshakeable Self-Belief—every successful entrepreneur has solid self-confidence and self-belief. Build yours so you can beat the nay-sayers and weather the storms with ease.

4) Generate Laser Focus—you don't get to the top by drifting off and thinking about other things. Get the full power of your unconscious mind behind your goals.

5) Develop an Unstoppable Work Ethic—anyone who tells you becoming a millionaire is not hard work has never done it. This session will make work your most enjoyable pastime.

6) Create Unbeatable Optimism—as you travel your

business path, you will come up against obstacles. There will be times when you wonder if you should give up. This session will give you a solid bedrock of optimism, so you just know it's going to work, even on the darkest of days.

UK based hypnotherapist Marissa Peer says that there are only three things you need to know about your mind: it likes what is familiar, it responds to the pictures in your head, and it gravitates to what you desire. Harness the power of your mind to create prosperous productivity by intensifying your desire, visualising success, and making productivity part of your daily ritual.

Along with hypnosis, creating a productivity vision board, saying daily affirmations, and writing at a regular time are just some of the many ways you can apply these three mind tools.

Program your subconscious mind for prosperous productivity and experiment with this powerful technique.

12

AFFIRM SUCCESS

Experience is the mother of all Knowledge.

~ Leonardo da Vinci

Leonardo was just like you and me. He made mistakes, faced many obstacles, and endured hardships—including envy, criticism, false accusations, exile, and the rejection and destruction of many of his most beloved works. He was human and experienced self-doubt like the rest of us.

There were times when he may have felt like giving up —and sometimes did. But his courage and persistence to remain true to himself in the face of adversity can inspire us all.

One of the secrets to his success, one that strengthened his will was his use of empowering affirmations. In his notebook, he urged himself on:

- I do not depart from my furrow

- Every obstacle is destroyed through rigour
- Obstacles do not bend me
- As you cannot do what you want, want what you can do
- I shall continue
- I am never weary of serving

RESILIENCE in the face of adversity is a critical determinant of prosperous productivity. Listed below are a few of the affirmations I use to empower my productivity. Which ones I use depends upon the current challenge I may be facing.

As you read my affirmations you'll notice I use the second-person pronoun (you). A recent research paper published in the *European Journal of Social Psychology* reported that task performance strengthens when you talk to yourself as You. This is also the way mind-programming experts such as hypnotherapists write their hypnosis scripts.

- You love writing and you love finishing your books quickly, productively, and joyfully
- Life is a challenge and it's full of obstacles, but they are really just opportunities to rise above. Life is a fun game and you don't let drama get in the way of your writing
- You are a pen in the hand of God sending love letters to the world. You co-create with Spirit and joy
- You are devoted to using your creative talents. You are open to it being easy and fun
- Your creativity heals yourself and others

- You are a channel for God's creativity
- Your dreams come from Spirit and Spirit has the power to accomplish them through you
- You have an array of highly developed skills to achieve success
- You are organised, intuitive and wonderfully creative and you cultivate an optimal state of mind for creative writing with a relaxed but focused mind
- You are the maestro, the composer, the director who brings together your own collection of writing skills to compose and create your own masterpieces. You're directing your subconscious mind to fully activate those skills now, to bring them together to the forefront of your mind, to help you create wonderful stories and books which will excite and inspire the people who read them
- You focus all of your abilities on your writing goals. Each day your writing flows easily and skilfully and the more you write, the easier and faster your writing will come. And you will be excited each and every day at the rapid progress you make
- Writing and expressing yourself is one of your gifts in this life and you choose to use this gift to the best of your abilities. You've developed all the skills necessary to be a successful writer. You now choose to activate and utilise those skills prosperously and productively.

WHAT AFFIRMATIONS CAN you create to sustain you in the face of self-doubt or questioning of the value of your efforts? How can you cheerlead your way to success?

Plant your affirmations deeper by framing them emotionally. This engages your heart-centre so that deeper, more resilient changes can take root.

13

FIND YOUR VIBE TRIBE

When you choose to step out of limiting thoughts and listen to the song in your heart, you'll find the people who want to share and celebrate the journey with you. You'll find your tribe.

~ Dr. Julie Connor, author

The simplest definition of a tribe is a group of people that share the same language, customs, beliefs—and aspirations.

As you've already discovered, sometimes to flourish you need to break free of your current tribe and find one that fuels your dreams and brings out the best in you.

Your vibe tribe is a great team of others—whether they be significant friends, partners, or family members, or those found online through wonderful Facebook groups and webinars.

Gathering a team of like-minded people will nourish your burning desire and elevate your success.

I found my author vibe tribe online. We have never met in person, but we stay connected and share success strategies via Facebook, and occasionally we link-up on video conferencing calls.

As I write this chapter, a member of my vibe tribe, Scott Allan, who is the author of many brilliant books about living fearlessly, sent me a PDF of his successful book launch strategy. This is a powerful example of being co-creators in one another's mutual success.

My vibe tribe also finds me—reaching out to me after enjoying my books. Many of my readers love to help me co-create prosperity by reading advance copies of my new books and contributing valuable feedback.

This feedback, and the positive reviews on Amazon and via the online communities I have created for my readers on Facebook, sustains me and encourages me to keep writing. I love hearing their success stories.

Other readers have helped me grow my vibe tribe by interviewing me on their podcasts and success summits. Recently, Sheree Clark, a fabulous and influential healthy-living coach based in the US, discovered my book *Mid-life Career Rescue: The Call for Change* and showcased it on American television. She also included an interview with me in her fabulous "What the Fork" summit. You'll find a link to this interview and the TV clip on my media page at www.cassandragaisford.com/media.

Successful authors and podcasters like Tim Ferris (tim.blog/podcast) and Joanna Penn (www.thecreativepenn.com) found their vibe tribes by following their enthusiasms. They created their vibes by following their passionate purposes to share what they learn with others.

Here's a few ways to find a vibe tribe:

Financial Rescue: The Total Money Makeover 41

- Scan Facebook for like-minded groups
- Enrol in a writing course—they often include a private members group on social media
- Create a Facebook community of your own—show up and encourage others
- Listen to podcasts which inspire you to become the best version of you—Joanna Penn's podcast is very helpful for "authorpreneurs." I also love Neil Patel's podcast for savvy marketing strategies: http://neilpatel.com/podcast. Tim Ferriss' podcast is also always inspiring: http://tim.blog/podcast.
- Join writers' groups and become an active member of writing bodies—romance writers, for example, gain huge encouragement from The Romance Writers of America, Australia, and New Zealand. These professional groups are dedicated to helping their members thrive. They offer courses to learn new skills from established authors; the chance to enter competitions where you can gain valuable feedback (or win!); conferences at which to network, meet agents and pitch your books—and much more encouragement.
- Check out Meetup.com and find a group of like-mined souls to meet up with in person
- Speak from your heart, write with passion and purpose, and send your love letters to the world via your books, blogs, podcasts, or other mediums, including social media

How can you develop an encouraging network of friends and acquaintances?

How can you remove yourself from people who don't encourage or support your dreams?

14

ASSESS YOUR CURRENT SITUATION

Get an accurate picture of all your outgoings and expenses. Consolidate debt. Seek financial advice if necessary.

Get a reality check on your future plans

Is there a current or future demand for your writing?

Could you create one?

What is the true cost of making a change?

Isolate costs against benefits: cash in against cash out.

How much money do you really need to spend and create?

15

EARN MORE

Think laterally to create cash flow.

A job doesn't have to be a full-time thing. Can you finance your career by doing a career-combo, working in a variety of different ways or for several employers?

As you've read, many people work at several jobs to earn extra cash.

Generate extra cash flow by increasing the money you earn

Some possible strategies include:

Negotiating a pay rise in your current position;

Taking on a new higher-paying role;

Or turning a hobby into cash flow.

New Zealand based, USA Today bestselling historical romance author Bronwen Evans, for example, took on a high-paying, high-pressure, one-year communications contract to allow her to take a year off so she could pursue her dream of becoming a full-time novelist.

16

SHARE THE LOAD

Who else has a stake in your success? Perhaps they may be able to inject more cash into your joint cash flow or pitch in and share the family load. New Zealand romance author Leanna Morgan asked her husband to take on the day-to-day family commitments so she could focus on her writing.

Today she's a USA Today bestselling author who sells up to 300 books a day and has legions of fans in America. She's also the CEO of her own publishing company. In just two years, Morgan has gone from an unknown writer to one who earns over $200,000 a year, allowing the mother-of-two to give up her job as a Libraries and Arts Manager to concentrate on her writing. She recently shared with me that her goal is to make a million dollars, and more, from her writing.

"If anyone had told me two years ago that I'd be able to resign from a job I loved to become a full-time writer and publisher, I would have smiled and thought they were slightly crazy. But believe it or not, that's what happened," she told journalist Anna Kenna.

"Her success has not been without sacrifice, including

little sleep and less time with husband Tim and her two children, aged 12 and 17," Kenna writes in her article.

"I'd be up at 5.30am, getting in a few hours of writing before work, and writing in the evening when everybody else was asleep."

So she could devote herself to writing, Leanna's husband Tim shared more of their responsibilities.

"Tim took over running the house and organising our children," Morgan says. "He did it to support me, but also because he could see the potential benefits of my success for the whole family."

Sharing the load, hard word and commitment have yielded success beyond her and her family's dreams.

"It's taken away the financial stress, allowed us to take a nice holiday and to look forward to a future we never considered possible," she says.

Find out more about Leanna Morgan here www.leeannamorgan.com and read the rest of this article, including why it's a brilliant time to be an independent author http://www.stuff.co.nz/entertainment/books/85799137/How-one-Kiwi-author-is-making-200-000-a-year-publishing-romance-novels-online

17

SEEK INVESTORS

Use other people's money to create the momentum you need. Remember there's good borrowing—borrowing to increase wealth, and bad borrowing—borrowing so you can consume more.

Most people spend all their spare income on non-asset-producing consumption.

Banks, family members and friends are all possible sources of investment income.

Sam Morgan, who established the on-line trading company TradeMe, convinced his dad to back him, and earned millions of dollars in return.

You may not pay back millions, but if your idea is sound, your investors can sleep at night knowing they will be repaid.

18

GET FUNDED

Many people and organisations offer sponsorship and various forms of funding to help people pursue their dreams.

Without the help of a grant from Creative New Zealand, author Lloyd Jones may never have written *Mr Pip*—the same book for which he won the prestigious and lucrative Man Booker Prize. The book was later made into a film.

Check out crowdfunding as an option, as *Heather Morris* initially did. Her attempts to finance her film script lead to a multi-national publishing deal for her book, *The Tattooist of Auschwitz*.

Max ensured he had a credit-line when times were buoyant. During the Coronavirus crisis of 2020 when banks reduced lending he had access to over $80,000 of credit. "It was a lifeline," he told me.

19

UTILIZE EQUITY

Burt Munro, whose story was made famous in the movie *The World's Fastest Indian*, mortgaged his home.

Could you use the equity in your own home to finance your career?

If you don't want to re-mortgage you could try asking for a mortgage holiday. Many banks allow 2–3 months of no mortgage payments.

As fashion designer Calvin Klein once said, "I took the risk of putting my money on the line for the company." Are you prepared to do the same?

20

REDUCE OUTGOINGS

Reduce outgoings. Review your current commitments and expenditure. Proactively look around to make sure you are getting the best deal possible on your insurance, mobile phone plans, mortgages and other regular financial commitments.

Take note of your savings and squirrel the extra money away for a rainy day.

John shopped around for a better deal on his household insurance and saved himself over $600 annually in premiums.

He also negotiated an instalment plan with creditors so that he could increase his credit debt repayments, saving over $5,400 in interest charges annually.

21

MULTIPLY YOUR INCOME STREAMS

When authorpreneur Kevin Kruse made the move to self-employment he decided to record his financial success, complete with the highs and lows by publicly sharing his income reports on his blog. While it may be out of date, there's lots of relevant information and inspiration for anyone about to embrace change here:

http://authorjourneyto100k.com/income-report-december-2015-and-full-year/

"Each month, for the last 12 months, I've chronicled my wins, losses and income," he wrote.

Like many business people, Kevin knew early on, that having a variety of income streams would help him manage cash-flow.

"I went into this whole thing knowing that to make the money I wanted to make I would need to diversify my income. I knew I'd need to spend time speaking, creating online courses, and marketing."

It is a common and successful strategy used by many business people, especially those working creatively.

New Zealand celebrity chef, Ruth Pretty is a chef, newspaper columnist, cookbook writer, wedding venue provider, caterer and cooking school tutor. The common theme? Her pursuits all centre around her passion for food.

Italian designer Giorgio Armani has a flourishing clothing empire, a swag of luxury hotels, a music production company, and an interior design business. And these are just a few of his multi-billion-dollar revenue lines.

Amongst other things, photographer Carla Coulson is a portrait photographer, magazine photojournalist, tutor, and travel photographer. Several years ago she diversified her business and retrained as a life coach and now offers location independent creativity coaching and wellness workshops. During the Coronavirus travel freeze she was happy she had planned ahead.

I am a self-empowerment author, coach, holistic therapist, romance writer, brand manager, and novelist of art-related historical fiction. I also write marketing materials (blogs, newsletters, website content etc.) for small businesses. As I mentioned earlier, I also train people to become location-independent certified life, career coaches and courage coaches.

Keeping ahead of the changing ways people were consuming books, I diversified my writing to include audio-book narration.

As my writing income grows I'm making a conscious decision to spend less time in some of these areas and more in others.

You may wish to focus on one income stream, but if this doesn't work for you, consider diversifying. This will help you ride any fluctuating financial currents.

22

MAINTAIN SOME BALANCE

Every now and then go away, have a little relaxation, for when you come back to your work your judgment will be surer. Go some distance away because then the work appears smaller and more of it can be taken in at a glance and a lack of harmony and proportion is more readily seen.

~ Leonardo da Vinci

Workaholism is an addiction for many passionate people. Others use overwork to medicate their unhappiness in other areas of their life—most commonly dissatisfaction with their relationships.

When you work slavishly, particularly at something you love, your brain releases chemicals called opiates which create feelings of euphoria. No wonder it's hard to step away!

Euphoria stems from the Greek word *euphoría*—the power of enduring easily. But consider what the state of endurance implies. Enduring implies force or strain, or gritting your teeth and bearing it at times. Force or strain with no respite leads to stress, overload, and burnout—robbing you of vital energy and depleting your millionaire mindset.

Many people find when they don't step away from their work they suffer disillusionment, and things that once filled them with passion, including their current writing project, no longer fills them with joy. Resentment builds and relationships with family, friends, and colleagues can also suffer.

Working addictively offers a short-term fix, but lasting happiness needs variety and nourishment. Being with family or friends, engaging in a hobby, spending time in nature, learning something new, helping others, or just being solitary will help you avoid burnout, nourish your brain, heart, and soul, improve your judgment, and restore harmony.

To be truly happy and successful, you must be able to be at peace when you are working and when you are at rest.

Leonardo da Vinci would often take breaks from his work to refresh his mind and spirit. While others claimed that he took too long to finish things, he knew the importance of replenishing his focus to maintain a clear perspective.

Here we are still talking about him over 500 years later.

Leonardo also valued sleep, noting in one of his journals that some of his best insights came when his mind was not working.

Even if you love the work that you do, and think your book is the greatest thing since man launched into space, it's fun to get away from it and have objective-free time to unwind and reset.

When you return to your work, your focus will be surer, your vision refreshed, and your confidence bolder.

Who are you when you are not working? Do you still feel successful? Do you feel worthy?

When was the last time you truly relaxed? Can you think of a time when you stepped away from your work and when you returned, your mind was clearer, your confidence surer?

Schedule time out—and be firm with yourself. Stay away from anything that feeds your addiction.

What can you start doing, stop doing, do more or less of? What benefits will flow from these changes?

23

PROTECT YOUR MENTAL HEALTH

I still have to sit down in peace and write the books.

~ J.K. Rowling

"I didn't quite resonate with some sections of the book like 'health,'" an advance reader of *Developing the Millionaire Mindset* wrote to me.

Tellingly, he also wrote, "Perhaps I was in a different emotional state."

So many people have not valued their health and then during COVID-19 realised they had compromised their immune systems ability to fight.

Jessie Burton, author of *The Muse and The Miniaturist*, powerfully sums up the importance of protecting your health—mentally, emotionally, physically, and spiritually.

Below is an extract from the vivid account she shared on her blog earlier in 2017 detailing how anxiety can sneak up on your:

"I looked my mental health in the eye and did not do enough to protect it. I burned out again, I suffered dehydration and a viral infection, but far worse, my anxiety came in huge and truly awful doses and, in the end, I had to cancel a few events.

I am well aware of the places I had to cancel events, and one day, I hope to make up for that in those places. It wasn't many, but I did feel terrible.

I truly love having readers, and I did the best I could, a four-month publicity tour, two continents, five events in three days kind of thing, but by the end of September, the scrutiny and analysis, repetition and a sinking of myself led to physical damage and a deep sense of alienation, panic and an indefinable loss.

The thing I want most to do in the world is write, and I agonised that if writing led to this kind of struggle, then what was the solution?" she asked.

Balance. That is the solution. And writing, more than talking about writing," she replied.

"It's too late for me to be an Elena Ferrante [an Italian novelist, best known for her *Neapolitan Novels*]. I have thought much about authority, invisibility, how to synthesise the experience of life into fiction in the best ways I can, the ways that feel truest and strongest and will make a reader go with me and say, yes.

A writer's selfhood vies with her need to make herself invisible, in order to freely inhabit a simulacra of multiple lives in fiction (aka Ferrante), and work without worrying about her own received persona in all of it.

A published writer has people pay to read the manifestations of her imagination, soul, and heart. "For me, that remains extraordinary. It will always be the dream transaction for me, but it is also the most exposing, the rawest, unavoidable, supremely important fact in my life that I have battled desperately to understand and get a handle on these past three years.

It's a rockier path, certainly, knowing you are going to be held publicly accountable, knowing that your personhood will be as relevant to your artifices when it comes to talking about the work.

I know I'm not alone in this battle and I am grateful to the other writers who have spoken to me about this on the way, sometimes reaching out without me even having to ask.

My own lack of anonymity when I publish is something I am coming to accept. I handed it over without even thinking about it.

I made a pact with the kindly devil with my eyes wide shut, but I do not regret it. Having my novels bought and read has been the best thing that ever happened to me.

Sometimes, however, the things that are best for us are not always the easiest. I do regret my inability to find my pause button, but maybe writing that regret here will enable me to locate that mysterious setting inside myself?

I want to write, and write well, and that's nearly all I ever want to do."

How can you prepare for inevitable success and avoid overload and overwhelm?

What mental health practices would make a tremendous difference to your sustained prosperity?

You'll find a few helpful reminders and strategies in the chapters which follow.

24

STRESS LESS

Productivity isn't about being a workhorse, keeping busy or burning the midnight oil...It's more about priorities, planning, and fiercely protecting your time.

~ Margarita Tartakovsky, blogger

As Jessie Burton's experience illustrated, when you are under too much pressure, take too much on and don't take time out, you tend to live your life on overdrive and on the verge of burnout.

When you're stressed you are less effective, make more mistakes, suffer more and are prone to illness.

Very often people turn to "medicine"—chemical highs, alcohol, and prescription drugs—to manage the symptoms.

But the reality is that these only offer temporary relief. They mask symptoms which, left unresolved, can set fire to everything you've worked so hard to achieve.

Fortify your resilience. Stop, take a break, rest, eat well, stay away from negative people, cultivate optimism, exercise, do things you love, play, spend time in nature, experience the quietness of solitude, and experiment with other effective stress management techniques.

Would you die for success? Destroy your relationships? Sacrifice your mental health?

What can you start, stop, do more or less of to keep your stress levels at a healthy optimum?

DIVE DEEPER...

You'll find more strategies to manage stress and build greater resilience in *Stress Less. Love Life More: How to Stop Worrying, Reduce Anxiety, Eliminate Negative Thinking and Find Happiness*. Available as an eBook or paperback.

25

YOU BOOZE, YOU LOSE

Drinking worked in the beginning: I felt wonderful, warm, and fuzzy...almost pretty...What I didn't know was that I was in a prison of my own making.

~ Colette Baron-Reid, intuitive & author

Alcohol and success don't make good marriage partners, but they're often fatally attracted.

Experience may have already taught you that too much booze muddles the mind, ignites aggression, reduces responsiveness, and ultimately depresses.

It's also hard to quit.

While you don't need to be a teetotaller, alcohol control will make you a better, healthier writer.

Many successful people limit their drinking or consciously decide not to touch a drop. Keeping their resolve often takes extraordinary willpower.

"I spent last weekend suffering from a hangover after too

many drinks on Friday night. It literally wiped my weekend and I didn't get any writing done," shares Joanna Penn on one of her blogs.

"I like a glass of wine but I'm not very good on it, and I was very angry with myself for going too far. I have a lot to do at the moment, so I need that time. For me, drinking alcohol does not serve my writing."

Author and public speaker Deepak Chopra gave up drinking. "I liked it too much," he once said. Steven King, after almost losing his family and destroying his writing career, managed to quit.

Julia Cameron, author of *The Artist's Way*, fought her way back from alcoholism. Anne Lamott, author of *Bird by Bird: Some Instructions of Writing and Life*, is a recovered alcoholic.

Other creatives like Amy Winehouse devastatingly never made it. At only 27, she died of alcohol poisoning on July 23, 2011.

Ernest Hemingway committed suicide led from alcoholism, depression, and mental illness. F. Scott Fitzgerald and poet Dylan Thomas also died from poor health related to the complications of alcohol abuse.

Destroying your career, ruining your relationships, sacrificing your sanity, and taking your life is a massive price to pay for your art, or a mistaken belief that to be creative you must drink.

The many benefits of reducing your alcohol intake, or not drinking at all, include:

- A stronger ability to focus on your goals and dreams
- Improved confidence and self-esteem
- Increased productivity

- Increased memory and mental performance
- Better control of your emotions
- Sweeter relationships
- Greater intuition and spiritual intelligence
- Authentic happiness

NOT EVERYONE HAS a battle with booze. Whether you cut back or eliminate alcohol entirely, the choice is ultimately yours. Only you know the benefits alcohol delivers or the success it destroys.

Try sobriety. Experiment with living an alcohol-free life.

Consider rejecting or limiting alcohol and replacing it with creativity based on your sober self.

You'll find plenty of help and inspiration in my book *Mind Your Drink: The Surprising Joy of Sobriety: Control Alcohol, Discover Freedom, Find Happiness and Change Your Life.*

26

FIGHT FOR YOUR DREAMS

Remember your dreams and fight for them.
You must know what you want from life. There is just one thing
that makes dreams become impossible: the fear of failure.

~ Paulo Coelho, author

Novelist Steven Pressfield called it as it is when he titled his non-fiction book *The War of Art*.

It's war out there with many opponents—time, temptation, distraction, economic uncertainty, family, work demands, and more.

Very often you may find that you are your own worst enemy and are either consciously or unconsciously sabotaging your success.

As Jessie Burton, a successful novelist who suffers from anxiety once said, "If you really want to see your work to completion you have to desire it more than you believe. You have to fight it, fight yourself. It's not easy."

To help overcome some of the many things impeding

your dreams, you must strive to acquire the following mindsets:

1.) **A willingness to persevere.** Many authors' first novels, and their subsequent ones, even when they were at the height of their fame, were rejected.

"Perseverance is absolutely essential, not just to produce all those words, but to survive rejection and criticism," J.K. Rowling once wrote.

2.) **An ability to handle criticism—even laugh at it.** At a writers conference I attended several years ago, Michael Cunningham, the Pulitzer Prize-winning author of *The Hours*, was told by a man, "I loved your first book but I hate this one. I really think you've lost it."

I was shocked and the audience was aghast. After taking a moment to compose himself, Michael, who is openly gay, smiled and said, "I'm sorry if we have to break up over this honey. I write the books I want to read. If you like it great. If not, that's fine too."

The audience laughed and Michael's light-hearted and humorous response only added to his appeal.

3.) **An ability to fear less.** Many authors are self-critical about their abilities. Some feel anxiety, others despondency. Elizabeth Gilbert, author of *Eat, Pray, Love*, once shared how she feared she would never write another #1 bestselling book. But she showed up and wrote more books any way.

She's used this same courage to announce that she is

now in a same-sex relationship with a woman who was diagnosed with cancer.

"Death—or the prospect of death—has a way of clearing away everything that is not real," she said. "In that space of stark and utter realness, I was faced with this truth: I do not merely love Rayya; I am in love with Rayya. And I have no more time for denying that truth."

In the end, what matters is being true to yourself and cherishing the dreams which feel most real.

"I stopped pretending to myself that I was anything other than what I was, and began to direct all my energy into finishing the only work that mattered to me," J.K. Rowling once said.

How skilfully are you fighting for your dream of becoming debt free and prosperous?

Other than finishing and applying the strategies in this book, what additional tools, support, or weapons could help you fight through the blocks and win your inner creative battles?

How can you stay true to your vision and keep everything real?

27
REMIND YOURSELF THAT MONEY IS NOT A MEASURE OF YOUR TRUE WORTH

Clarify what's important to you. As Richard Branson said, "I don't work for money, that's too shallow a goal."

Lucky for him his passion for having fun has netted him millions—as it has for James Patterson and other prosperous authors.

Whatever path you choose, be sure to work with love. Sonia Choquette, author of *Your Heart's Desire* echoes this view:

"When you work with love you draw others to you. Embrace this truth. The reason for this is that love is the highest vibration on earth. When you work with love people feel it, are helped by it, and return to it. That's why love is the best marketing tool around. Because it is so attractive, it pulls right to you what you need."

28

THE MONEY OR YOUR LIFE

His Holiness the Dalai Lama, once said, "Choose a job that allows the opportunity for some creativity and for spending time with your family. Even if it means less pay—it is better to choose work that is less demanding, that gives you greater freedom, more time to be with your family and friends, engage in cultural activities or just play. I think that is best."

This really spoke to me and was one of the primary reasons I chose to scale back my successful international consultancy. Time is more valuable to me than money. I can always find ways to get more money, but it is impossible to find more than 24 hours in any one day.

Be careful what you chase. Is it more money, or a better quality of life? With planning, it just may be possible to do both says Timothy Ferriss in his bestselling book, *The 4-Hour Work Week*.

His central premise is to automate everything so you can live and work independently, free from a fixed location. If this is something that appeals to you I highly recommend picking up a copy of his book.

We'll also dive deeper into simple but savvy productivity

strategies in Book Two, of The Prosperity for Authors series, *Productivity Hacks: Do Less & Make More*.

In this book, you'll learn how to work less and produce more, including powerhouse productivity tools you can harness to help you finish what you start, create new books and take them to market so you can sell them faster.

If becoming a location-independent author is not your gig you'll find plenty of inspiration in my other career and life changing books. Check out my author page on your favourite online bookstore, and in the 'Also by the Author' section toward the end of this book.

29

KEEP LEARNING

I love those who can smile in trouble, who can gather strength from distress, and grow brave by reflection. 'Tis the business of little minds to shrink, but they whose heart is firm, and whose conscience approves their conduct, will pursue their principles unto death.

~ Leonardo da Vinci

Contrary to what some people may believe, taking time out to boost your motivation and self-belief is an extremely cost effective and productive use of time.

As one person wrote to me recently, "I just took an hour and watched your interview with Ande Anderson on the *Truth about Prosperity* summit thank you, it was once again inspirational and motivating. I am whisking along on my new idea, getting stuck, getting unstuck, tripping over, getting up and all the while loving every moment. There is so much to learn."

Similarly, a person who had read the first book in the series wrote, "WOW. I can't wait to read the whole book.

These books just keep on giving me the motivation and a constant feeling of being connected with others while working away on my own. Very cool."

Here are just a few ways to fuel your verve:
- ✓ Conferences
- ✓ Podcasts
- ✓ Ted Talks
- ✓ Seminars
- ✓ Books
- ✓ Webinars
- ✓ Workshops

How can you fuel your passion, belief motivation, and tenacity to succeed?

What do you need to learn more of, less of, stop or start learning?

Make investing in continual learning part of your success strategy.

Dive Deeper...

Empower your millionaire mindset and think your way to success; find out how in book one of the Prosperity for Authors series, *Developing A Millionaire Mindset*. Available in print and eBook.

Discover how to accent the positive, change your brain with music, cultivate hope, chase the light and develop patient perseverance.

Have you downloaded your free book?

Download the free *Passion Journal Workbook* here>>https://dl.bookfunnel.com/aepj97k2n1

You'll find tips to follow your passion to prosperity.

AFTERWORD

"Know what you want and try to go beyond your own expectations. Improve your dancing, practice a lot, and set a very high goal, one that will be difficult to achieve. Because that is an artist's million: to go beyond one's limits. An artist who desires very little and achieves it has failed in life."

~ Paulo Coelho, in *The Spy*

"Your thoughts, feelings, and beliefs are always engaging the fast field of pure potential," writes intuitive author Colette Baron-Reid.

Focus on your best life—regardless of any unfavourable or challenging outer conditions imposed on you by the physical world.

Whatever your current situation have faith that with will, determination and implementing savvy debt-reduction and income boosting strategies you will survive and thrive. You have divinely inspired talents to sow, nurture, harvest, and share with others.

Do the work, be a channel for inspiration, create big

magic—thoughts really do become things and you will reap what you plant in your field of dreams.

Adopt a millionaire mindset and get out of your own way—dream big, be audacious, take inspired action, and fear less. Live more and experience the extraordinary life that awaits you. The power to create a life of prosperous significance lies within you.

Remember the truth about prosperity.

It's deeper than whether you have millions in the bank, three houses on the French Riviera, drive a limoncello coloured Lamborghini or become a New York Times Bestseller.

Good fortune and prosperous productivity can mean counting the blessings for the seemingly simplest things—things that sadly too many of us take for granted. Your good fortune may include:

- Enjoying good health and mobility
- Being loved and loving in return
- Tapping into your infinite potential
- The ability to say, think, do, and write what you truly feel
- The ability to enchant and inspire others with your words
- Healing the world—one book at a time
- Money in the bank to cover the necessities of life
- Feeling happy with yourself
- Fulfilment
- Living authentically
- Being debt-free
- Making an extraordinary living from your writing

… Or something else.

What matters most is not how you define fortune, luck, prosperity, or whatever else you choose to name success. What matters is that the end result is meaningful to you.

If you continue to feel, think, and believe prosperously, then this unknown and unpredictable phenomenon will manifest in favourable outcomes—for you, those you love, and those drawn to you because of the beauty, power, and magic of your words.

If you infuse your life and work with your energy, power, talent, and essence, who knows—100 years from today somebody may well be writing a book about you and the legacy you left.

You may think the outcome has to happen in a certain way, on a certain day, to reach your goal. But human willpower cannot make everything happen. Spirit has its own idea, of how the arrow flies, and upon what wind it travels.

It may not happen overnight, but if you follow your heart, maintain your focus, and take inspired action, your time will come.

I promise!

If by some strange twist of fate, it doesn't, at least you'll know you tried. A life of no regrets—now that's worth striving for.

To your prosperity
With love

PLEASE LEAVE A REVIEW

Your feedback encourages and sustains me and I love hearing from you.

Show your support. Share how this book has helped you by leaving a REVIEW—Even a one-liner would be helpful.

I recently received an email from a reader who said, *"Your books are a fantastic resource and until now I never even thought to write a review. Going forward I will be reviewing more books. So many great ones out there and I want to support the amazing people that write them."*

Great reviews also help people find good books.
   THANK YOU

PS: If you enjoyed this book, do me a small favor to help spread the word about it and share news of this book with your tribe on Facebook, Twitter and other social networks.

ABOUT THE AUTHOR

Cassandra Gaisford, is a holistic therapist, award-winning artist, and #1 bestselling author. A corporate escapee, she now lives and works from her idyllic lifestyle property overlooking the Bay of Islands in New Zealand.

She is called 'the queen of uplifting inspiration' and is best known for the passionate call to redefine what it means to be successful in today's world.

Cassandra is a well-known expert in the area of success, passion, purpose and transformational business, career and life change, and is regularly sought after as a keynote speaker, and by media seeking an expert opinion on career and personal development issues.

Cassandra has also contributed to international publications and been interviewed on national radio and television in New Zealand and America.

She has a proven-track record of successfully helping people find savvy ways to boost their finances, change careers, build a business or become a solopreneur—on a shoestring.

Cassandra's unique blend of business experience and qualifications (BCA, Dip Psych.), creative skills, and wellness and holistic training (Dip Counselling, Reiki Master Teacher) blends pragmatism and commercial savvy with rare and unique insight and out-of-the-box-thinking for anyone wanting to achieve an extraordinary life.

ALSO BY CASSANDRA GAISFORD

Transformational Super Kids:

The Little Princess
The Little Princess Can Fly
I Have to Grow
The Boy Who Cried
Jojo Lost Her Confidence

Mid-Life Career Rescue:

The Call for Change
What Makes You Happy
Employ Yourself
Job Search Strategies That Work
3 Book Box Set: The Call for Change, What Makes You Happy, Employ Yourself
4 Book Box Set: The Call for Change, What Makes You Happy, Employ Yourself, Job Search Strategies That Work

Career Change:

Also by Cassandra Gaisford

Career Change 2020 5 Book-Bundle Box Set

Master Life Coach:

Leonardo da Vinci: Life Coach
Coco Chanel: Life Coach

The Art of Living:

How to Find Your Passion and Purpose
How to Find Your Passion and Purpose Companion Workbook
Career Rescue: The Art and Science of Reinventing Your Career and Life
Boost Your Self-Esteem and Confidence
Anxiety Rescue
No! Why 'No' is the New 'Yes'
How to Find Your Joy and Purpose
How to Find Your Joy and Purpose Companion Workbook

The Art of Success:

Leonardo da Vinci
Coco Chanel

Journaling Prompts Series:

The Passion Journal
The Passion-Driven Business Planning Journal
How to Find Your Passion and Purpose 2 Book-Bundle Box Set

Health & Happiness:

The Happy, Healthy Artist

Also by Cassandra Gaisford

Stress Less. Love Life More
Bounce: Overcoming Adversity, Building Resilience and Finding Joy
Bounce Companion Workbook

Mindful Sobriety:

Mind Your Drink: The Surprising Joy of Sobriety
Mind Over Mojitos: How Moderating Your Drinking Can Change Your Life: Easy Recipes for Happier Hours & a Joy-Filled Life
Your Beautiful Brain: Control Alcohol and Love Life More

Happy Sobriety:

Happy Sobriety: Non-Alcoholic Guilt-Free Drinks You'll Love
The Sobriety Journal
Happy Sobriety Two Book Bundle-Box Set: Alcohol and Guilt-Free Drinks You'll Love & The Sobriety Journal

Money Manifestation:

Financial Rescue: The Total Money Makeover: Create Wealth, Reduce Debt & Gain Freedom

The Prosperous Author:

Developing a Millionaire Mindset
Productivity Hacks: Do Less & Make More
Two Book Bundle-Box Set (Books 1-2)

Miracle Mindset:

Also by Cassandra Gaisford

Change Your Mindset: Millionaire Mindset Makeover: The Power of Purpose, Passion, & Perseverance

Non-Fiction:

Where is Salvator Mundi?

More of Cassandra's practical and inspiring workbooks on a range of career and life-enhancing topics are on her website (www.cassandragaisford.com) and her author page at all good online bookstores.

ACKNOWLEDGMENTS

This book (and my new life) was made possible by the amazing generosity, open heartedness, and wonderful friendship of so many people. Thank you!

Sir Edmund Hillary often said that even Mount Everest wasn't climbed alone. A great achievement, or in my case a good book, is a product of collaboration. This project has, at times, loomed larger than the highest mountain in the world. I could not have persevered without the tremendous encouragement from a wealth of supportive and talented people.

To all the amazingly interesting clients who have allowed me to help them over the years, and to the wonderful people who read my newspaper columns and wrote to me with their stories of reinvention—thank you.

Your feedback, deep sharing, requests for help, and inspired, courageous action continues to inspire me.

My thanks also to my terrific friends and supporters. And, of course, I can never say thank you enough to my family, particularly my parents and grandparents, who have instilled me with such tremendous values and life skills.

My daughter, Hannah—I wish for you everything that your heart desires. Without you, I doubt I would ever have accomplished all the things I have in my life.

Thank you.

STAY IN TOUCH

Become a fan and Continue To Be Supported, Encouraged, and Inspired

Subscribe to my newsletter and follow me on BookBub (https://www.bookbub.com/profile/cassandra-gaisford) and be the first to know about my new releases and giveaways

www.cassandragaisford.com
www.facebook.com/powerfulcreativity
www.instagram.com/cassandragaisford
www.youtube.com/cassandragaisfordnz
www.pinterest.com/cassandraNZ
www.linkedin.com/in/cassandragaisford
www.twitter.com/cassandraNZ

And please, do check out some of my videos where I share strategies and tips to stress less and love life more—http://www.youtube.com/cassandragaisfordnz

BLOG

Subscribe and be inspired by regular posts to help you increase your wellness, follow your bliss, slay self-doubt, and sustain healthy habits.

Learn more about how to achieve happiness and success at work and life by visiting my blog:

www.cassandragaisford.com/archives

SPEAKING EVENTS

Cassandra is available internationally for speaking events aimed at wellness strategies, motivation, inspiration and as a keynote speaker.

She has an enthusiastic, humorous and passionate style of delivery and is celebrated for her ability to motivate, inspire and enlighten.

For information navigate to www.cassandragaisford.com/contact/speaking

To ask Cassandra to come and speak at your workplace or conference, contact: cassandra@cassandragaisford.com

NEWSLETTERS

For inspiring tools and helpful tips subscribe to Cassandra's free newsletters here:
http://www.cassandragaisford.com

Sign up now and receive a free eBook to help you find your passion and purpose!
http://eepurl.com/bEArfT

COPYRIGHT

Copyright © 2019, 2020 Cassandra Gaisford
Published by Blue Giraffe Publishing 2020

Blue Giraffe Publishing is a division of Worklife Solutions Ltd.

Cover Design by Cassandra Gaisford

All rights reserved. No part of this publication may be reproduced, distributed, or transmitted in any form or by any means, including photocopying, recording, or other electronic or mechanical methods, without the prior written permission of the author or publisher, except in the case of brief quotations embodied in reviews and certain other non-commercial uses permitted by copyright law.

Neither the publisher nor the author are engaged in rendering professional advice or services to the individual reader. The ideas, procedures, and suggestions contained in this book are not intended as a substitute for psychotherapy, counselling, or consulting with your physician.

Copyright

The intent of the author is only to offer information of a general nature to help you in your quest for emotional, physical, and spiritual well-being.

Any use of information in this book is at the reader's discretion and risk. Neither the author nor the publisher can be held responsible for any loss, claim or damage arising out of the use, or misuse, of the suggestions made, the failure to take medical advice or for any material on third party websites.

ISBN PRINT: 978-0-9951137-3-2
ISBN EBOOK: 978-0-9951137-4-9

Second Edition

www.ingramcontent.com/pod-product-compliance
Lightning Source LLC
Chambersburg PA
CBHW030452010526
44118CB00011B/908